SHARICE'S BIG VOICE

A NATIVE KID BECOMES A CONGRESSWOMAN

SHARICE'S

BIG

VOICE

A NATIVE KID
BECOMES A
CONGRESSWOMAN

by Sharice Davids
with Nancy K. Mays

illustrations by
Joshua Mangeshig Pawis-Steckley

HARPER
An Imprint of HarperCollinsPublishers

This is a picture of me and my mom, the night I was elected to Congress. When I see this, I think how amazing it is I won. I think how amazing it is I even *tried* to win. When I was young, I never thought I'd be in Congress. And I *never* thought I'd be one of the first Native American women in Congress.

During the race, I heard from a lot of doubters. They thought I couldn't win based on what I look like, who I love, and where I started.

But here's the thing: *Everyone's* path has obstacles—some more than others; everyone faces challenges and people who doubt them. (Sometimes we even doubt ourselves!)

Everyone's path looks different.

Let me tell you a little bit about mine.

When I was young, I liked to talk. *A lot.* (I still do!)

I talked to my family, my friends, my friends' families.

I talked to neighbors, people shopping in the store, people working in the store.

I wanted to know things about people, like Did they move often? Had they ever seen martial artist Bruce Lee kick through a wall? And did they also hate onions on their pizza?

My mom likes to talk too. Watching her, I saw how a good conversation can make people happy. You start as strangers, but then you share ideas and learn about each other.

Maybe you learn they've moved four times.

They love Bruce Lee.

And, unlike me, they don't care if their pizza comes with onions. (I still care. A lot.)

Sometimes, I got in trouble for talking too much. (Okay, more than sometimes.)
My teacher even moved me by her desk, but that didn't stop me.
"Sharice," she finally said, "move out to the hall to finish your work. You can't talk out there!"
But she was wrong. I just talked to whoever passed by!

One day, a boy in my class grew upset, so upset he bolted out of the classroom.

"Sharice," my teacher said, "can you get him to come back?" When I found him outside, I did what I always do—I started talking. Then *he* started talking, and I listened. That was all my friend needed, and we went back to class.

I was getting better at listening. I learned that listening gives people room to be themselves, to feel angry or sad or happy.

I discovered that the best way to **LEARN** about people is to **LISTEN** to them.

My friends at school were confused about me because I looked different from them. They always asked, "What are you, Sharice?"

So one day I asked my mom, "What am I?"

"You're Native American," my mom said. (After she told me that wasn't a nice question to ask people.)

"We're members of the Ho-Chunk Nation," she said.

I learned my mom was removed from her family and told to pretend she wasn't Ho-Chunk. Our Nation is mostly in Wisconsin, where my aunts and cousins live. We're related to the Winnebago tribe in Nebraska.

We used to be all one people, but long ago, the US government forced tribes to move away from their homelands.

I also learned we call ourselves

PEOPLE OF THE BIG VOICE.

(Which obviously fits me well!)

My big voice came in handy every time I started a new school. My mom was in the army for twenty years, so we moved back and forth between Germany, Kansas, and Missouri.

At every school, I made friends by talking and listening. I knew a good conversation could break down walls. (Just like Bruce Lee.)

In Germany, a soldier taught me martial arts for free. I wanted to keep taking lessons when we returned home, but my mom couldn't afford them.

So I watched Bruce Lee movies—all the time. He could do a roundhouse kick, a palm strike, and a flying arm bar!

I ran around the house PUNCHING and KICKING, trying to copy him.

While my mom was being strong and fierce at work, I was strong and fierce at home.

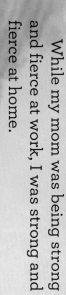

When I was thirteen, I went to my mom's work for a special ceremony. She had earned a promotion to a higher level in the army—sergeant first class.

My mom asked *me* to pin the special sergeant patch on her uniform. I watched her stand at attention in her army fatigues, an American flag behind her. I felt so proud.

FOCUSED and FIERCE.

CONFIDENT and KIND.

A person who serves others.

It took years for her to earn the promotion. I knew how hard she worked. And I knew I wanted to be like her when I grew up.

I learned how to work hard by watching my mom.
I sold newspaper subscriptions and worked in a pizza restaurant. (No onions on mine!)
Later I paid for college by working in a fast-food restaurant, making burgers, cleaning
bathrooms, and calming upset customers.
I learned you can't always fix someone's complaint—when you're out of mustard,
you're out of mustard! But you *can* listen.
And you can do *something* to make them feel better. (Like maybe free ice cream?)

In college, I used part of each paycheck for martial arts classes so I could finally learn to fight like Bruce Lee.

JUJITSU.

TAE KWON DO.

CAPOEIRA.

I could land a punch and defend against a palm strike. But more importantly, I learned that when I worked hard at something, I got better at it—even if I couldn't see it right away.

I trained every day—for years. Finally, I was ready for my first mixed martial arts fight.

I was nervous, but I knew I was prepared. Standing in the ring, I thought about my training, all those hours practicing, and then . . . the bell rang.

We met in the middle of the ring, and I pounced on my opponent.

In less than a minute, I won my first fight—and with my favorite move, a triangle hold.

The crowd cheered! With my arm raised high, I realized it felt good to win. But it felt even better knowing I won because I'd worked so . (You know how that feels, rig.)

At the same time that I was fighting in the ring, I started a journey with a different kind of battle. I decided to enroll in law school so I could work to make our US laws more just and fair.

I didn't know anyone who was both Native American and an attorney.
I didn't even know any attorneys! But martial arts taught me not to be
afraid of new challenges.

A friend told me about a program for Native Americans preparing to
be lawyers, and I signed up! It was the first time in my life I'd sat in a
classroom surrounded by Native people. It felt powerful.

No one in that room asked, "Sharice, what are you?"

Once I had my law degree, I worked for a big law firm. But it didn't feel right. It didn't feel like my path.

So I moved to a reservation in South Dakota. I saw that my Native friends there didn't have the kind of opportunity I had in Kansas, so I used my legal skills to help them start businesses. I learned a lot living there, and my life is better for it.

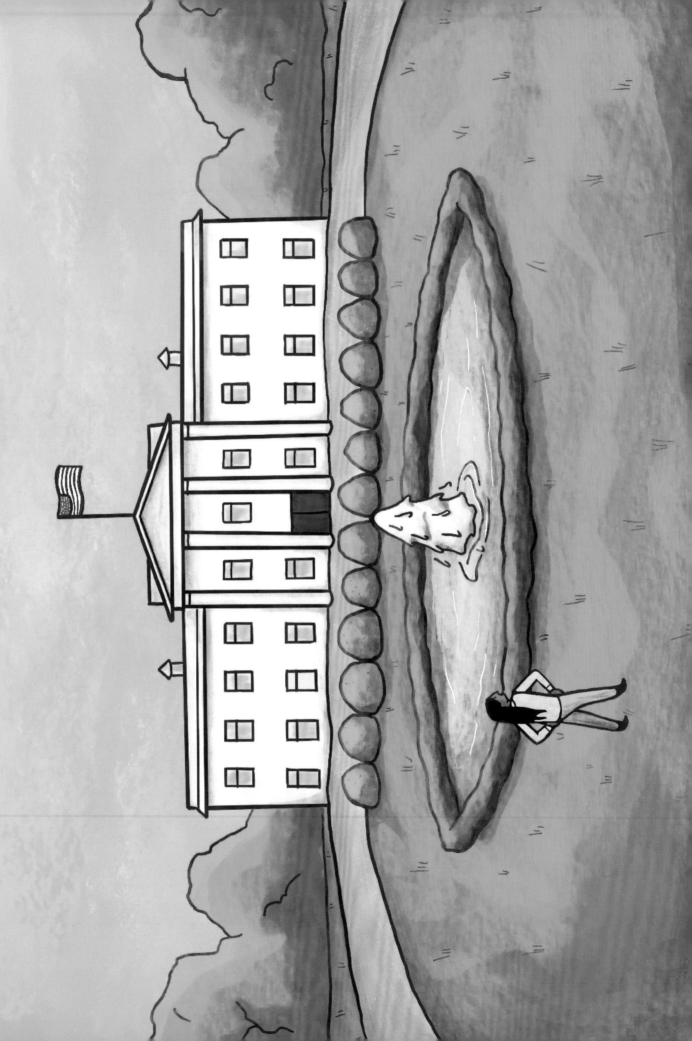

Working with Native American tribes, I saw that the people who make up the American government don't always see how the laws they make impact the people they represent. I wanted to change that, so I went to work in the White House.

There, I saw how laws were made, but I *didn't* see people who looked like my family. I *didn't* see people who'd grown up like me.

What if that changed? I wondered.
What if everyone's voice was heard by the people making our laws?

That's when I had a bold, brave idea that would need my big voice, my ability to listen, and my ability to take a punch. (Turns out, a lot of punches.)

Can you guess what I'm talking about?

I decided to run for US Congress!

Our government needed different voices—and more people who would listen.

I had doubters. People who didn't think I could win. Or that I should even run. (But do you think I listened to them?)

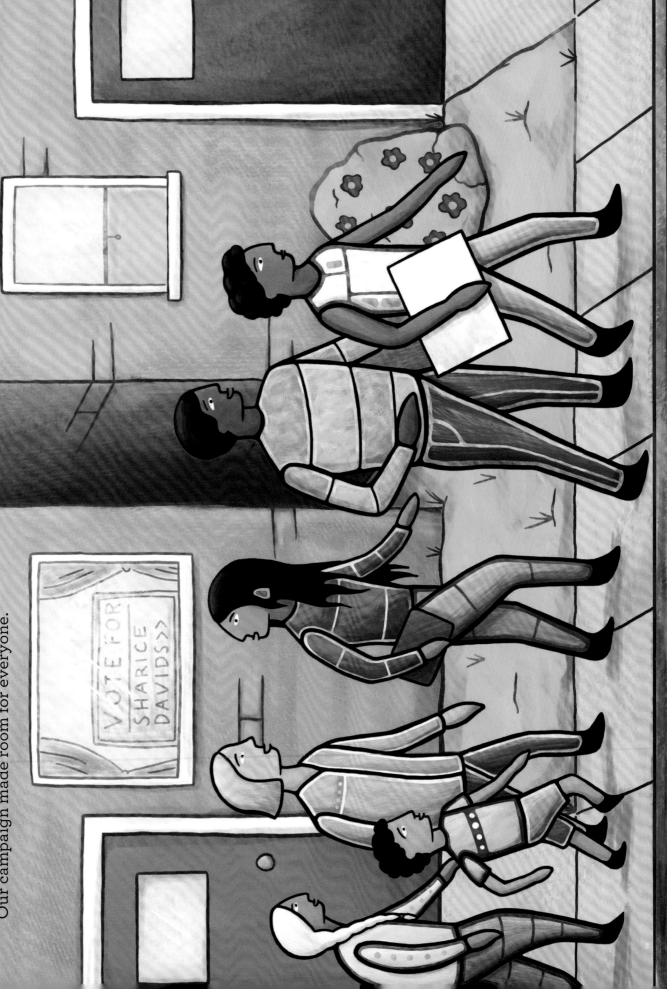

In the beginning, the campaign team was small enough to fit around a kitchen table. But as we walked through neighborhoods, more people joined us.

Our campaign made room for everyone.

VOTE FOR
SHARICE
DAVIDS >>

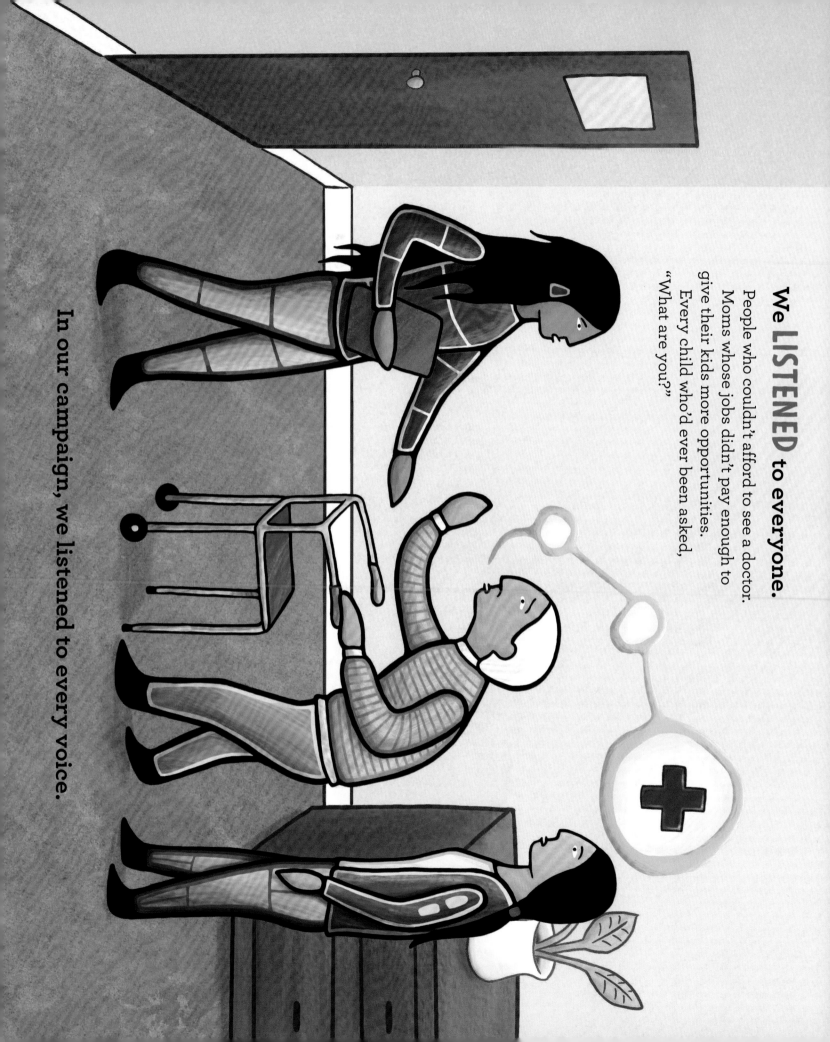

We **LISTENED** to everyone.

People who couldn't afford to see a doctor.
Moms whose jobs didn't pay enough to
give their kids more opportunities.
Every child who'd ever been asked,
"What are you?"

In our campaign, we listened to every voice.

The night of the election, I hoped we would win. I knew how hard everyone had worked on the campaign. I knew how important it was for their voices to be heard.

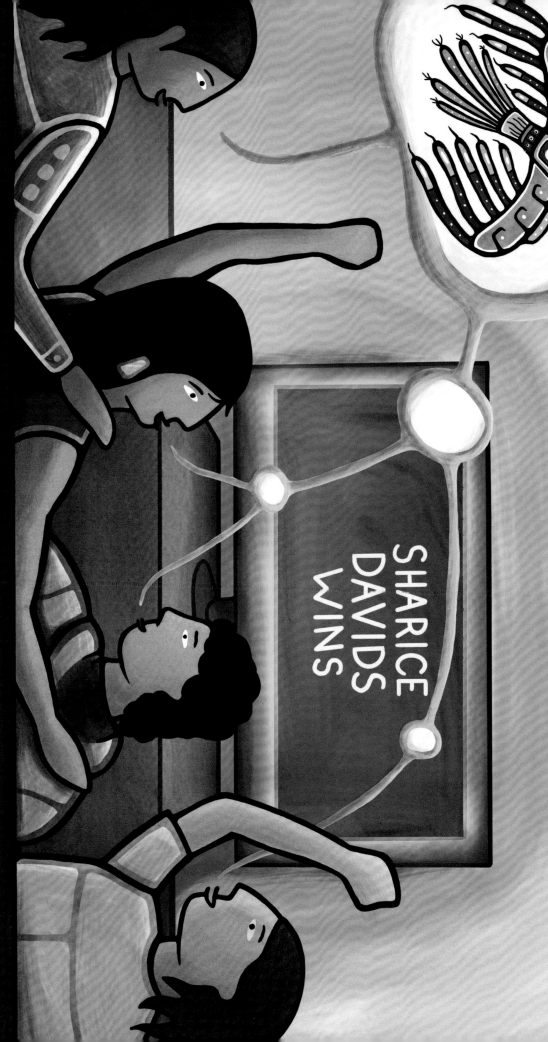

I watched the election results on TV in a small room with my best friend, my family, my campaign team, and my partner. We laughed, talked, and ate macaroni and cheese. When the results came in, I'd won—by a lot!

I walked out of the small room into a ballroom and saw the smiling faces of all the people who'd helped on the campaign. As they cheered and clapped, I climbed onto the stage with my mom and we lifted our arms. We did it! I felt like everyone—every voice—was rising up with me.

SHARICE
DAVIDS
WINS

Growing up, I never would have guessed my path would lead to Congress. I didn't know I would be one of the first Native American women in Congress and the first lesbian representative from Kansas.

Everyone's path is different, and wherever yours takes you, maybe the lessons I learned can help.

Be open to challenges.
Work hard and you'll learn a lot.
Listen to people. (But not the doubters!)
Use your big voice to fight for your beliefs.

And always remember:
YOU DESERVE TO BE SEEN—AND HEARD.

AUTHOR'S NOTE

Hello! I'm glad you're here, reading our story. I say "our" story because, even though the details are about my life, this is everyone's story. Mine. Yours. Our dog Nala's. (Okay, maybe not hers.)

Here's what I hope our story conveys: That each of us has our own path—and the most important thing in the world is to be true to your own journey. That journey is going to have ups and downs, people who doubt you and people who cheer you on. Focus on the supporters. Be grateful for their help. I am.

I also hope you realize the power in your choices. As you know by now, I went to law school. Often, people have said to me, "I bet law school changed your life." But the truth is that the school didn't change my life. My choice changed my life. Your choices will change yours as well.

And law school may not be your choice. Your choice may be working with animals or learning magic tricks or being a singer. The point is, you get to decide what success means for you. That's your choice and only yours. And remember that whatever your path is, you're changing the world just by being here.

It took me a while, but I'm really glad I found my big voice. If you haven't already, I hope you find yours too, because I can't wait to hear what you have to say.

Your friend,

Shauna

Also, remember to take naps. You're going to need a lot of energy to change the world.

ARTIST'S NOTE

One of the most exciting aspects of working on this book was finding in myself the illustration style that best honored the relationship both Sharice and I have to our past, present, and future as Indigenous people on Turtle Island. As an established Ojibwe Woodland artist, I create my work to honor my Anishinaabe family and all people who would like to enjoy this art form and find a connection to themselves along the way.

When I read Sharice's story, it resonated deeply with me because she speaks so openly about how she grew up disconnected from her nation. And it also exemplifies Sharice's journey home by connecting with her culture and community. We share a similar history of displacement, and I think her story is an empowering example of resilience. It is such an honor to heal through artistic exploration of another Indigenous person's success.

We come from generation upon generation of being silenced, being made to conform to a culture that is not our own. As a young Indigenous person growing up a decade ago, I could never have dreamed of accessing these types of powerful two-spirit Indigenous narratives. Sharice's is a historically and culturally significant success story for all young people. It is my desire that these illustrations do justice to the work she has done for the next seven generations of people here on Shkagamik-kwe (the Anishinaabe word for Mother Earth). My hope is that whoever reads this book will witness her resilience and understand that they can do anything they want to do in life. The world is a warmer, brighter place when we grow into who we are. Thank you so much for allowing me to brighten these pages with my love and artwork.

ABOUT THE HO-CHUNK by Jon Greendeer, former president of the Ho-Chunk Nation

According to our oral tradition, we were here long before the woolly mammoths and saber-toothed tigers, spanning several ice ages, and we remain a vibrant Nation today. But if you only know about Indigenous people from old Westerns, you may have a lot of incorrect ideas. You may even think we existed only in the past. We are very much here in the present and will be here in the future as well.

Just like that of any group of people, the story of our people isn't a static one—we evolve, react, adapt, and respond to changing situations. Our story is one of resilience, courage, and incredible resourcefulness fueled by a warrior tradition and our way of life, or as we refer to it, our *woošgą*.

OUR LANGUAGE

Aho. Hizakisana hinikaragiwino. That's how you say "Hello. I greet every one of you" in the Ho-Chunk language. Ho-Chunk means People of the Sacred Voice.

The name of our people comes from the words *hoora* (voice) and *wakącąk* (sacred). We are named for our language, which was given to us to use during the time Mąą'ųna (Earthmaker, the Creator) finished his creation on Grandmother Earth. He wanted the beings he created to speak directly to him, so he blessed them with a voice so sacred that he could hear it whenever it was spoken. It is said that during hard times, neighboring tribes would travel to the Ho-Chunk to ask them to speak to the Creator in hopes that their messages would be heard. Our language is rich and descriptive. For example, the word for "thank you," *pinagigi*, literally says "you've done well for me." We have been told through ancient oral tradition that as long as our language carries on, so will our people.

The Ho-Chunk go back to time immemorial, long before documented history. Our traditional lands spanned the region now known as Wisconsin, Minnesota, Iowa, Missouri, and Illinois. We have always been hunters.

We've also fished, foraged for wild foods, and farmed as we do today. Our connection to our ancestral lands is one of our most sacred, deeply held values.

THE HO-CHUNK CLAN SYSTEM

The Ho-Chunk have a clan system that is divided into two parts, the Sky and the Earth clans. The Sky clans include the Thunder, Warrior/Hawk, Eagle, and Pigeon clans. The Earth clans include the Bear, Wolf, Water Spirit, Buffalo, Deer, Elk, Fish, and Snake clans. Each clan assumes certain traditional roles within the community. For example, the Sky clans have judicial responsibilities, the Water Spirit clan protects the water, and the Bear clan serves as police. The Warrior clan has special responsibilities to protect the people and lands during battle.

But the Ho-Chunk have a strong warrior tradition that extends across all the clans, not just those who belong to the Warrior clan. Today, many of our people enlist in the military and remain on the front lines fighting for social justice and as leaders in their communities. Being a warrior is part of our DNA as Ho-Chunk people. We celebrate the exploits of our warriors with ceremonies. In our society, veterans (especially combat veterans) have special privileges and rights. Veterans can name children, present eagle feathers to young dancers at special times, have the honor of raising the flag, and are permitted to speak at any public meeting.

We are fortunate that we still have our language, our kinship and clan traditions, and our warrior tradition. We came close to losing it all. . . .

OUR TRIBAL HISTORY FROM THE 1800S ON

Beginning around the 1820s, white settlers and miners wanted our rich lands in southwest Wisconsin and northern Illinois. Ten thousand people flooded into

our homeland. These interlopers destroyed our crops, reduced our hunting territories, and took our valuable lead. In 1830, US president Andrew Jackson signed the Removal Act, a law that allowed the removal of Native Americans from one land to another. More and more settlers were moving west, and they wanted our lands. Again and again we were removed at gunpoint and forced to go to new places over the course of about thirty years: Iowa, Minnesota, South Dakota, and finally the Winnebago reservation in Nebraska. Conditions were brutal— sometimes we were packed into railcars so tightly that people could only stand, in subzero temperatures.

Despite horrible conditions not just on the journey but also in the new places, the Ho-Chunk were able to adapt. But we have deep ties to our ancestral land. We consider ourselves an extension of our Grandmother Earth. So wherever

we were, those who could started walking back to Wisconsin or, in some cases, making canoes and paddling back. Those of us who returned had to live like fugitives on our own lands, hiding in the woods. The governmental policy of keeping the Ho-Chunk off their land was a failure. Eventually, a law was passed allowing the Ho-Chunk to stay on our own land. Parcels of land that hadn't been claimed by settlers were ceded back to us.

Then we had to face a different challenge just as wrenching as the removal policies: the attempt to wipe out our identity as Native people. Starting in the 1870s—and lasting into the 1970s—Native children were forced to leave their families and live in residential boarding schools, where they were horribly punished for speaking their languages or practicing any traditions. Many Ho-Chunk parents actually stopped giving their children Native names at birth because they feared the young children wouldn't remember not to say their names and would be punished.

Today, the original Ho-Chunk have two distinct federally recognized sovereign Nations: Those who stayed in Nebraska are members of the Winnebago Tribe of Nebraska. Those of us who returned to Wisconsin belong to the Ho-Chunk Nation. The Ho-Chunk Nation has about eight thousand members in Wisconsin, in the Chicago and Minneapolis areas, and scattered throughout the United States and beyond.

OUR WARRIOR TRADITION

We still proudly uphold our warrior tradition. And Sharice Davids is a warrior.

Being a warrior is a position of huge responsibility. In her role in the US Congress, Sharice is charged with fighting for the protection and security and rights of all. The Ho-Chunk people have a great deal of pride that she is one of our own, and we will always and forevermore see Sharice as the leader and warrior that she was born to be.

In honor of my mom and all the
strong Ho-Chunk women before us.
—S.D.

To my mom and dad, love you both.
—J.M.P.-S.

Sharice's Big Voice: A Native Kid Becomes a Congresswoman

Text copyright © 2021 by Sharice Davids
Illustrations copyright © 2021 by Joshua Mangeshig Pawis-Steckley
All rights reserved. Manufactured in Italy.

ISBN 978-0-06-297966-7

The artist used Procreate to create the digital illustrations for this book.
Design by Chelsea C. Donaldson and Carla Weise
21 22 23 24 25 RTLO 10 9 8 7 6 5 4 3 2 1
❖
First Edition